Eyes of A Miracle

Illustrated Lyrics of Faith

Based on the song by Joe Guadagno

Hear the song on Spotify!

Hear the song on Apple Music!

Hear the song on YouTube!

by Joe Guadagno
and Victoria Winifred

Eyes of A Miracle:
Illustrated Lyrics of Faith
©2025 Joe Guadagno and Victoria Winifred.

Published by The Enrichment Connection.
Paperback ISBN: 979-8-9915289-8-6
1st Edition

All Rights Reserved. No part of this book may be reproduced or transmitted in any form or by any means whatsoever without express written permission from the author, except in the case of brief quotations embodied in critical articles and reviews. Please refer all pertinent questions to The Enrichment Connection at enrichmentconnection@gmail.com.

DISCLAIMER: This work is based on a song "Eyes of A Miracle," written and recorded by the author, Joe Guadagno. Any resemblance to actual persons, living or dead, outside of biblical context, is purely coincidental. This work also includes passages from the Bible. All Scripture quotations are from the King James Version (KJV), which is in the public domain.

All of Joe Guadagno's music is available on most major music streaming platforms, either under his name or his band's name, JGnFriends.

To all who have experienced the miracle of welcoming a child into their lives.

The first time that we saw this perfect new creation,

no words came close to properly express our pure elation.

Our eyes were filled with wonder, our hearts were filled with love

for this precious little one entrusted to us from above.

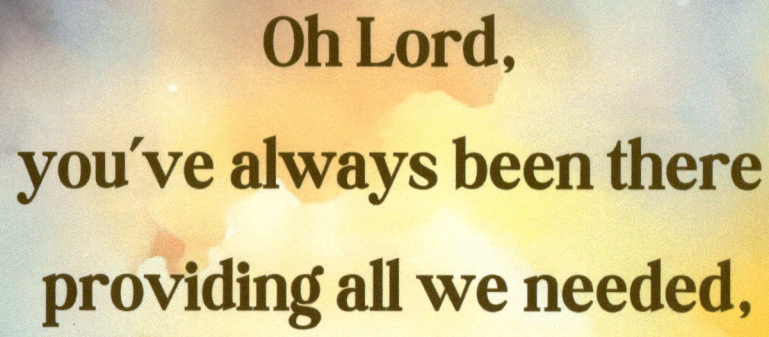

Oh Lord,
you've always been there
providing all we needed,

but in this gift
our greatest
dreams
have been
exceeded.

Each time our child is in our arms
and we gaze into that face,
we're reminded of
the endless bounty of your grace.

We thank you, Lord,

for loving us so much,
and sending us
your touch
from heaven.

and with these lips proclaim to all the world your gospel story.

We praise you, Lord.
When we look into those eyes,
Lord, we realize

Biblical Verses About Children (KJV)

Psalm 127:3
Lo, children are an heritage of the LORD: and the fruit of the womb is his reward.

Psalm 139:13-14
For thou hast possessed my reins: thou hast covered me in my mother's womb.

Proverbs 22:6
Train up a child in the way he should go: and when he is old, he will not depart from it.

Isaiah 54:13
And all thy children shall be taught of the LORD; and great shall be the peace of thy children.

Jeremiah 1:5
Before I formed thee in the belly I knew thee...

Matthew 19:14
But Jesus said, Suffer little children, and forbid them not, to come unto me: for of such is the kingdom of heaven.

Questions for Discussion:

Understanding the Experience:
What was your first reaction when you saw your child?

Exploring Emotions:
How did becoming a parent change your perspective on life and love?

Personal Reflection:
Can you describe a moment when you felt overwhelmed by the wonder of your child? What emotions did you experience?

Thinking Deeper:
In what ways has your child's arrival made you reflect on your own beliefs, values, or spirituality?

Applying the Message:
How can you carry the sense of wonder and gratitude expressed in this book into your everyday life as a parent? What practices might help you maintain this perspective?

Reflecting on the gift of having a child, take a moment to write your own prayers or reflections.

_____

_____

_____

_____

_____

_____

_____

_____

_____

_____

Enjoyed This Book?
Check Out More Titles by Victoria Winifred.
All Available on Amazon

Illustrated Lyrics of Faith Series:

The Prodigal Son: Illustrated Lyrics of Faith (27 pages.) Based on the timeless biblical account, this book explores themes of decisions and consequences, repentance, and forgiveness with beautiful illustrations and Bible discussion tools for the whole family. It also includes links to the song on which the text is based. This book is a great gift for pastors and churches.

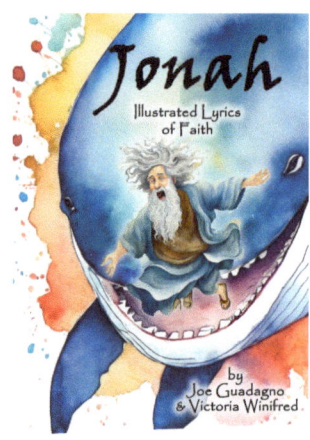

Jonah: Illustrated Lyrics of Faith (26 pages). Based on the book of Jonah, this book explores the essence of his wayward journey, wild adventure with the big fish, and redemptive return. It features beautiful illustrations and Bible discussion tools for the whole family. The text includes links to the song on which it is based. This is a great gift for pastors and churches.

More in this series coming soon!

Smoky Mountain Bear Adventures: A Series for the Whole Family!:

Come Home, Papa Jed:
Smoky Mountain Bear Adventures (Book 1) (36 pages.)
Papa Jed Bear has been out fishing for a long time, and Momma Daisy Bear, along with cubbies Huck and Lily, set out on a search. Along the way, they meet other forest friends, who all rally to help. Stunning illustrations on each page!

Papa Jed's Christmas Eve Awakening:
Smoky Mountain Bear Adventures (Book 2) (47 pages.)
Papa Jed and his family venture out on Christmas Eve and follow the North Star for a special reminder of the season's meaning for all creatures on Earth. Beautifully illustrated from start to finish!

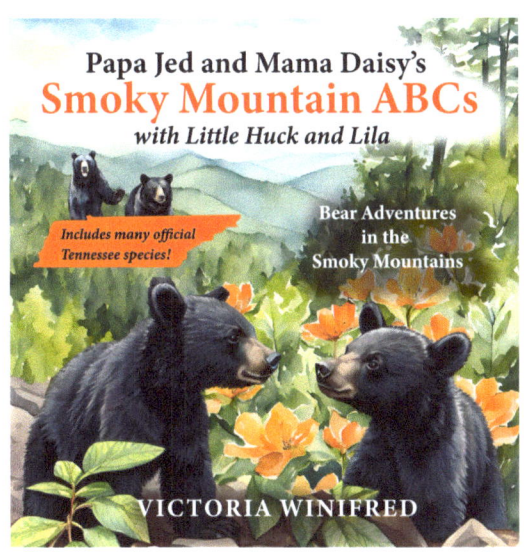

Smoky Mountain ABCs:
Smoky Mountain Bear Adventures (Book 3) (28 pages.)
For ages 2-6, cubs Huck and Lila remember what their parents taught them about the Smoky Mountains to help them learn their ABCs. Fun animal facts and many official Tennessee species are highlighted. Breathtaking artwork on every spread!

More in this series coming soon!

More by Victoria Winifred:

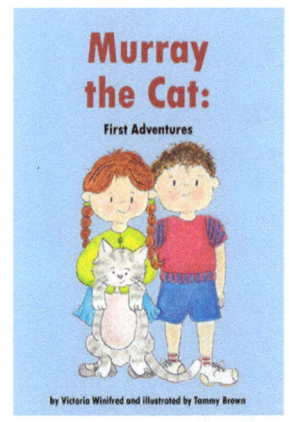

Murray the Cat: First Adventures (Grades 1-3)
(36 pages.) An older feline is searching for a new home and finds the family of his dreams. But first he has to convince them that they all belong together. This is an early chapter book with adorable illustrations, comparable level to the Henry and Mudge, Mr. Putter and Tabby series. Proceeds help increase placements of animals in shelters.

Abbie's Angel: A Christmas Puzzle (Grades 2-5)
(86 pages.) Abbie's Christmas spirit is taken away right before the holiday break. A mysterious angel appears to help the Cozy Chess Club hunt down the clues to get it back for her in time for winter break. Learn four Christmas chess checkmates! Comparable level to Magic Treehouse/A-Z Mysteries/ Goosebumps series.

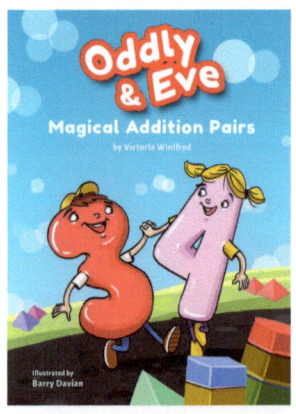

Oddly & Eve: Magical Addition Pairs (Grades Pre-K-2)
(36 pages.)
Oddly, an odd number, feels sad because he can't find a total that makes him happy. But with help from a wise professor and a friendly even number, Oddly opens his mind and makes an amazing discovery. Introduces addition in a fun, engaging fairy tale with positive life lessons about teamwork!

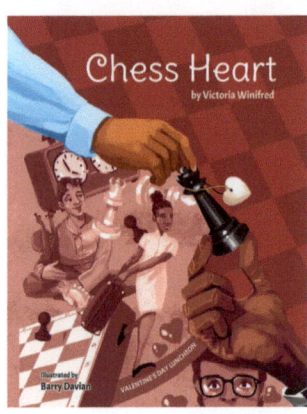

Chess Heart (Grades 3-5)
(30 pages.) In a small Tennessee town, a mysterious woman with a chessboard has long intrigued the locals. When she appears at the school's community luncheon, the third graders ask her to teach them the game. She realizes that the part of her life she thought was lost is closer than she ever imagined. Perfect teacher/classroom gift!

A Sample of Awards Earned by the Author:

LITERARY TITAN
BOOK AWARD

Pinnacle Book Achievement Award

HONORING EXCELLENCE
Children's Book International
WINNER
CHILDREN'S LITERATURE

First Prize
AMERICAN WRITING AWARDS
WINNER
2022
Children's Fiction

KIRKUS REVIEWS
Awards & Accolades
OUR VERDICT
GET IT

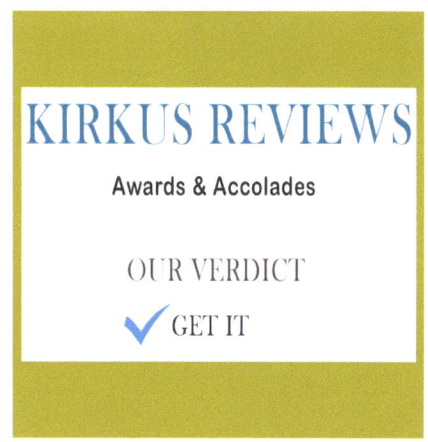

Do you want the author of this book,
Victoria Winifred,
to visit your school?

Just ask your teacher, principal, or media specialist to email her at VWinifredWriter@gmail.com or at VW@VictoriaWinifred.com

Victoria Winifred offers both in-person and virtual author visits and will work with your school to make one happen!

I hope you enjoyed this book! I'd greatly appreciate it if you would take a few moments of your time to leave a review of it online.
Thank you so much!

Visit me at
VictoriaWinifred.com